MW01113335

Pimp in Distress

The Untold Story of a Pimp of This Pimp Life Style

by

Pimp in Distress

RoseDog❈Books
PITTSBURGH, PENNSYLVANIA 15238

The contents of this work including, but not limited to, the accuracy of events, people, and places depicted; opinions expressed; permission to use previously published materials included; and any advice given or actions advocated are solely the responsibility of the author, who assumes all liability for said work and indemnifies the publisher against any claims stemming from publication of the work.

All Rights Reserved
Copyright © 2016 by Pimp in Distress

No part of this book may be reproduced or transmitted, downloaded, distributed, reverse engineered, or stored in or introduced into any information storage and retrieval system, in any form or by any means, including photocopying and recording, whether electronic or mechanical, now known or hereinafter invented without permission in writing from the publisher.

RoseDog Books
585 Alpha Drive
Suite 103
Pittsburgh, PA 15238
Visit our website at *www.rosedogbookstore.com*

ISBN: 978-1-4809-6857-8
eISBN: 978-1-4809-6880-6

07/21/2015

Pimp in Distress

The Untold Story of a Pimp of this Pimp Life Style

To all

"Viewers and Listeners this Book is Rated XX Read at your
Own Risk'

~~~

I did'nt grow up a pimp I grew into what I born with. I had a rough childhood, and it tought me to be what I am. Never fight who you are, and never be afraid to be what you are destined to be. It all started when I was seven years old in school the first sighn that I was different was when I was kicked out at the 3rd grade cause of the girls wanted me to be their pimp. My mother was a hoe in so many words, I hate to admit this but it was true and I understood this the older I got. My father was a pimp and did not hide the fact. Pimping was in my jeans at an early age. I seen a lot of things between them that a child my age should have not been seeing. I was exposed to a lot of things, this made me tough and gave me the tools that I would soon need later in life. What they were was carried on down to me cause this was all I saw, I was brought up in this lifestyle and never made excuses or blamed anyone for the way I was this turned me into what I am today, a man that stand alone and set my own trends I never followed the incrowd. I never planed to be a pimp growing up, this is something that your born with, it's in your jeans. This is something that your born with, something that's inside of you. It was in me. I believe this was because of my child hood which I really didn't have like the other kids because I was not like the other boys and girls. I did'nt dress like the other boys and girls or my brothers, and I carried myself different from them, at that point I knew I was different and there was something special inside of me that only I knew and I would soon find out as I got older. My mom worked long hours, days and nights, my dad had left home and was'nt around. My stepdad at this time worked many hours too, but was often left to watch us most of the time until my mother would arrive. It was me and my brother at the time, it would start from the time we got home from school. He would whip us for no reason at all. This was almost like a daily routine for us. I was locked in the closet for hours until I would submit or it was time to eat. He would always do this when our mother was not around, and it would stop right before she got home. Some days I really did'nt want to come home because I knew what was to come the moment he arrived. My brother would be tied up by one leg and beaten, when he would finally let me out I was told to sit on his lap with my penis out and he would put his mouth on it and proceed to malaste me, I never liked what was being done to me, but was over powered and restained when I fought back. We were even forced to call him dad, he was no dad to us. Sometimes he would give us money for the store as if nothing happen. Almost as if he was trying to bribe us for what he had done to us. By the time my mother got home he would act as if nothing had happen. When my mother would arrive she would go to the kitchen and begain to prepair dinner, that's when I would pull her to the side and try to tell her what had been going on while she was at work. She would slap me and call me a liar for saying that, I had no one to talk to not my mother, not my brother because the same thing was happing to him. I had no one to turn to, so I had all this bottled up inside of me for many years, and I believe this is the reason for many of my problems today. I've seen my mom beaten right in front of us, there was no one there to help her, and nobody to help us. This also ruined my brother later in life as well, once the word got out that we were trying to escape we were sperated. At this time it made me question, was this happing to all the kids, was this normal, I was just a child trying to figure out why this was happing and thought I was the blame, but no child is the blame for any type of abuse, I was a victom. Soon I was sent to live with my grandmother who then raised me from the age of seven. At that same age my grandmother saw me fucking her cow against the gate in the back yard on her plantation, but I wasent the only one I was just the one to get cought, and instead of telling me that was wrong she said that I was no good and that I had to leave her house and take your little hoe, who was my girlfriend at the time with you and don't come back cause you are not like the other boys, cause you are a little hoe. My little hoe had one child when I met her I had 3 boys and one girl by her, and came to find out she had been malested too. In my opinion this brought us closer together. She was kicked out of school for the same reason I was and now I understood why she acted the way she did and why she was like she was. All her friends was hoes as well so they got toghether and went out hoeing and got enough money to buy a 1949 ford. By that time I was 12 years old then I went back to my grandmother house and she told me the same thing to leave her house beacause I was a little hoe. So me and my hoes got in my 1949 ford and stat driving with no where to go, so we stoped in every town and started prostituting until we gathered up enough money to reach Chicago. I met another girl who was in the same life style I was in and thought me a lot. She had a lot of girlfriends who was just out having fun, I did'nt even know I was pimping. Then we turned that into money, we were just having fun. Who knew that this was the profession I would grow up into. This was my first sighn that pimping was in my blood from a young age. It was time to be a man, cause I never had a childhood.

Upon leaving Missippi on our way to Chicago we were pulled over by the police in which our car was taken for under age driving I was only 13 years old at the time, shortly after we were taken to jail where I would spend the next 3 weeks until our court date on which I was released on a I bond. Once leaving we were all in need of some mony and was seeking work, we needed money quick fast and in a hurry, 50 some of us started picking apples to earn some money while the others sold themselves as prostitutes. All our hard work finally paid off and we were able to aford another car, but was not at the leagal age to do so until I found an older gentleman to puchase it for us with the money we had all saved up I had difernt jobs over the time such as picking apples, machanic and worked on the farm whatever made us money to support ourselves.i soon ran back into my brother who was headed down the wrong path, he had begain to stealing, and was in and out of jail. From stealing our mothers car, radiators, car tires, whatever he could get his hands on, until that one day we were almost shot and killed for trying to steal a man's radiator out of his car, I had a bad feeling about this from the start, this was not the life for me. He continued down this path and is in prison til this very day. I still love him a wish him nothing but the best we were just on too different paths of life at the time. I learned a lot at a young age and had to grow up fast in order to survive in this world.at this time it wase'nt just me it was 12 of us just trying to survive and make it to Chicago, I also experianced raciasm during this time as well, also on way to Chicago we were chased from a resturant for trying to purchase some food, and chased off by 5 to 10 white males with bats, we got as far as we could until running out of gas and approached by a state trooper who purcased the gas for us and told us to never show our face on this side of town again. I finallly arrived to Chicago at the tender age of 16 all the way to Illinois. When I got to Illinois I pulled into a gas station and a black limo pulled up beside of me saying they all like my style and they took me into their home and began to teach me and train me the game, the ins and outs and thouht me how to sell drugs by my hoes. Their I was to put herion on all the girls to sell to their tricks"''''' at that time I did'nt know what I was doing cause I never had any experiace with drugs or prostitice before, I thought they were all my best friend and I did what they wanted me to do. On this day I was on the street and ran into a young man who told me who I was really dealing with drug lords and north side mob, so I got mad at my friend because I thought he was just talking bad about my friends yet I believed in my friends and carried out their mission to the fullest. At that time I was just 16 years old, my first time ever being away from Mississipi with no education about what I was doing with them gangs, 10 years later I finally leared what they were all about I asked them to let me out of the gang they told me it was too late because I was one of them now. On this day they called me in for a meeting that was going to be there pimp to prosttute girls for them around the world, they wanted me to train all the girls to prostitue, they even made up new id cards cause they were from over seas so they would be able to work all aroud the world, and they even had their own doctors to have there tubes tied so thet couldn't have babies, and they dressed me in all the pimp clothes,gave me money and everything I needed lots of cash so I could transport the girls around the world to diffrent vicks, aftr that they sat me down and let me know that I was 1n the drug game and that I was here to stay and I was to train all the girls how to prosttitute and controll all the drug sells, they wer bringing in a 100 or more girls at a time for me to train them which meant having sex with 300 plus hoes and then they started to put 100 girls under me for prostitutin and to sell drugs, in 6 months I prostituted 300 plus hoes to prostitute world wide, they range from Chicago to China, there were 100 with me in Chicago and the other 200 were spreaded throughout the country. I used many different cover up's to hide what I was really doing. This was to explain some of the money that was coming in and I was getting a check for it as proof I never really needed the money I was living a double life, the life of a working man by day and a pimp by night. I worked for gm motor company. Upon me getting the job one of the girls hustled up enough money for me a brand new tool box and all the tools for me to start the job, with all the right tools I was hired on the spot. I had nothing but I was always able to find work, until I had enough money to start my own. During this time the hoeing never stoped, the girls continued to do what they did and brung in the money and I did the same. The very next day I was stoped and had mt gun on me that I had carried was found, I was taken to jail and charged with a concealed weopen. I contacted my hoes and was bailed out that same day with a thousand dollar bond. I had hoes but still did'nt know how to use them. It was like having solidiers that don't shoot. They were always there and showed up whenever I needed them. Over the time we had begin to get bigger and had started to make a name for ourselves. I was never into the drug part of the game but was talked into this by the hoes 1n order for us to make double the money. They would sell the drugs and I would collect the money, sounded like a plan to me but I had no idea for what I was in for. The drugs brung in more hoes and the hoes brung in more vicks. During this time my brother was released from prison and he decided to join my organization. We controlled the sales, and made sure all the money was collected for all the hoe houses for count. Upon our last stop I had a strange felling run across me. We entered the apartment building looked up and noticed a women at the tpo of the stairs holding a 38 straight at us. She pointed it at me and pulled the trigger, it went click, click, click, the gun had jamed. We ran up the stairs as fast as we could, my brother grabed the gun and said it was loaded. I had been saved again, I should have been dead on the spot. Someone was keeping me here. My brother took her and held her until she paid up the money. Who knew this would be the same woman to almost kill me not once but twice. This same women somehow broke into my house when I was asleep and I was beaten in my sleep, nose broken, and stabed. Later I was found and rushed to the hospital, and just in the nick of time too. I had lost over 70 percent of my blood and was in need of a blood transfusion, they did'nt think I was going to make it. Through the grace of god I pulled through and had another chance at life. I never wished bad luck upon anyone, but like the saying goes what goes around comes around is very true, because this same women would later over dose on the same drugs that she stole and now has suvere brain damage. It's funny how things works in life sometimes. After my recovery I started all over again, evrything new, new hoes, new contacts and drugs coming in. I started it all from the ground up. In order to get my name out there I started making house calls, straight from the phone to your door, straight delivery. I was charging 150 dollars an hour. During this I have been put in bad situations doing this. Some of the girls to advantage of this method and started robbing some of the vicks when they got them out of their clothes. Soon as they would drop their panths they would steal the wallets and run out the door where I would be waiting for them, some of them took the guys whole panths. This was not my style of buisness and I had to set rules for them to go by. I did'nt get into this game to rob the vick but to please him. Doing it this way would keep us in buisness and they would just hand us the money instead of robbing them. Some of the hoes were good at what they did and made a lot of money doing it. One of my best hoes would serve 7 to 8 vick at one time, when she would get through with one she would start on the next and had request from all over. I would drive all the hoes to the destination and I knew how much time was paid for and time over would be extra, nothing personal just buisness. Then I became one of my best customers and lost eveything to the drugs and the game didn't want me anymore because I was now a drug addict and became homeless and was sleeping outsde, under vidocks with no wher to go. So the drug rehab sent me back to my mothers house wher I started a fire and burned the whole house down because she would'nt give me money foe my drugs, so then they put in jail where I spent 6 months for arson, there is wher my morther decided not to press charges and I was released. After my release my mother drove me to the train station and told me to go back where I was from because I was no good. Then enterd myself into 3 or 4 difrent rehabs to get me clean and finish what I had started this time on my own. There my mother sent me clothes, then I put own the best clothes and dressed to impress and went back to the streets where I got noticed and begain my own orinization everything on my own this time. I had work lined up for me every time I hit the streets someone would notice me and ask about my hoes. If you talking the right price then we was in buisness and I would let you know that I had a hoe for you upon your description and she would be sent to you or depending upon where you was he could come to her. I hit a lot of little cities as well such sa Detroit, Philly, and all through Michigan, I had had hoes everywhere. I had 50 hoes assinghned to each state and had them all put up in the best of the best of condos and I supplied the room and board. That was just me, and how I did things. Top notch the best of the best and I treated them the same way. Whre ever there was a hoe willing to work I had them. At this time 1 was still stationed in Chicago, but often visited these various cities if need be, just to see if everthing was going as planed. I never announced that I was coming I would just show up. Everyone plays the role when they know your coming. Even when we were not in the same state or city we still moved as one. They would not move from that condo until they got my call to do so and I had a vick for them. We were a team and was a well oiiled machine if I may sy so myself. Team work makes the dream work, and Ihad no plans of stoping now. To name a few more of the cities included Minnasota, St.Paul, Nabraska, and all of Jackson Missiippi. I had begain my pimping down south and pimped all the way to Chicago, stoping in each town, city, or state we went through. With all of these hoes and dealing with all of these places 1t was hard to keep up and stay in contact with one another. We schecheld meetings and month and had to travel back and forth directly to one another. In my organization I ordered all of my hoes to wear rubber gloves or plastic gloves they would carry with them when arriving to a vick. They all had a supply they carried with them. I did this cause I wanted nothing to be able to be traced. This was in case anything came up and the vick tried to give up one of my hoes, they could not be traced. Anything they touched from a cup, sink, the toilet, or even the vick himself, they would leave no fingerprints. They would wear them from the moment they got there to the moment they left. I have seen a lot of pimps taken down from this. I have seen a big time pimp taken down from a single Mcdonald's cup and the FBI were watching him. He threw away the cup and the they went and got it, they got the fingerprints from the cup and traced him down from this. That made me think and gave me the idea for this, and made sure this wouldn't happen to me or any of my hoes. You always have to stay ten steps ahead of the game and always stay thinking how the police would think. Never have a set routine or a set pattern. Always stay ready, and you want have to get ready. With this mindset I promise you want fail. This was also pre cell phones days. When the cellular pagers were invinted we operated through them. I purchased pagers or beepers as some called them for all of my hoes. I even had extra pagers for the hoes that would later come. When they would come and past all of my test, I would give them a pager, program my number and have it activated. They all had my number and knew what time it was when they seen that number. We also had codes for the some of the vicks that was sent to the hoes telling them what they had to do. I would hit the streets and get maybe 30 or 40 vicks ay a time just by walking down the street. When I reached a certain amount 1 would contact my hoes. When I contact them I would tell them how many vicks I had for them, where they had to travel, and what they had to do. Some of the vicks might be in the same city, and they would'nt have to travel at all the vick could come to them. When they got my page they would get to nearest payphone and return my call, then I would proceed to tell them the details. Before this 1 was calling their names, then the bigger we got this became risky and we couldn't call out each others nme on the streets, because you never knew who was watching or who was listening. Each of my hoes that was from over seas I gave a second chace of life to by changing their whole idenity. They would no longer be the same person when they arrived to the states. I begain to get more and more girls from all over and it had become hard to keep up with all of them and there names. I started calling my hoes mud cats. I used the nickname mud cats for all of my hoes. This worked for a while,then the vicks started getting confused and did'nt know ho they were asking for if they all had the same name. Saying I had mud cat last time. It was time to change it again. I had to think of a way to keep track of all these hoes and be able for the vicks to know the difference beween them when requesting one. I dicided to use numbers this time. Numbers one through three hundred and so on. Now they would be strickly known by number no longer by their government or mud cats. I had the number of each girl tattooed on the back of their necks. When they show me the number I knew who they were. This was better for me and less confusing for the vicks, all they had to do was ask for a number or tell me what they were looking for and I would know what number to call up. This would also throw off the police if they seen this, to them it was just another tattoo.everyone had a job to do. Most of the hoes that had crossed the border were all set up with leagal jobs around the city through different people I knew on the inside and in higher places. This was the first step for them to become a legal citizen. I gave them all new id cards, mailing addresses, driver lisence, and even was able to change their mother's maiden names. I did all of this incase anything came up or they were stoped and questioned by the police nothing could be traced. I was in big buisness with these hoes from over seas, and they were bringing in more girls every day. Eighty percent of my buisness was coming in from over seas. The other twenty percent was here in the united states. I was able to change their whole identification, and give everything new. They were now legal US citizens. I could only do this for the hoes that was from over seas, the ones that were already

from here and born here were already u.s citizens. Most of them
held down the jobs that were given to them and worked them
well as a cover up to hide the fact of where all of this money
was coming from. They were receiving legal checks. They
worked mostly days and some early evenings in orde to leave
the night open. They still had to maintain a flexable schedule
in case they had to be called in. If I had a vick that was spending
four or five thousand dollars and had requested for them, they
had to be there. They had to be able to maintain their job and
still be able to prostitute, this was a twenty four hour job. Getting jobs foe all of my hoes was not just to have exta money, but
for them to earn a legit paycheck. This would also set them up
for the future and when they retire they could have some type
of pension coming in. Something to fall back on. I always
thought about life after pimping and instilled this into my hoes
too. Some of them maintained their jobs for five or ten years,
some still have these jobs. I also did the same when I started
working at general motors. I was the only person that showed
up to work in a three piece siut dressed from head to toe. I was
picked up and dropped off at work in a limosine, my co workers
could/nt understand where I was getting the money to do all of
this. I was making more money than the boss of the company.
I was making fifty dollars an hour as a certified machanic. No
matter how I dressed I always showed up to work on time and
did my job. I held this job down for almost ten years and still
was pimping on the side. I receive a pension from general motors every month to this day I live off of. I was living the true

14

meaning of a double life in order to secure my future. throughout all of these cities, of course we had our share of run in's. I had more hatred shown against against me in Chicago. Run in's where other pimps wanted my hoes and offered them money undr the table to work for them, they refused and always came back and told me. I never loss a single hoe. I had loyalty and trust in my organization and that could not be broken. Some of the hoes would get vicks on their own just by walking down the street, they never handeled buisness themselves,they would give the vick my information and we would talk buisness and my rates. I would give the hoe a little extra for being honest and bringing in their own vicks but that was not their job. If they were interested in one of my hoes then we could talk. We all came together when it was crunch time. Everybody did their fair share and supported each other. They supportde themselves and gave me gifts and things of that nature all the time. They have bought me cars, suits, jewelry, and homes. They also was the ones that bought my first very own pimp cup, black and gold with the diamond trim custom made just for me. I was on the streets that very day when a car had pulled up beside me and presented me a box that had my pimp cup in , which I still have to very day. I have been honored with many different things and I thank all of them. I have been honored and invited to many of the pimp and players ball which I chose to never attend. I was thankful for the invite but that was never my style. I was totally different from all of the pimps and players that were there. They did it for the reconition, the glitz and glamour.

It was a way of life for me and had no time for anything that was'nt making me money, I stayed away from things like that and tried to avid the spot light as much as I could. We you went to things like that you were exposing youself and letting everyone what you were and look at me had it all and remained undrcover for a long time and out lasted all of them. The true definition of a pimp is a well dressed man who is a agent for prostitute or prostitutes. You have to know this before you can call yorself one. It is in you or not, cause if it's not in you the hoes will end up pimping you. Evryone has different views of what pimping is and what it really means. I have never forced or did wrong to anyone, I only lead them in the direction that they were headed to begain with. I never asked, they asked me. I never sold anyone but myself. The game is cold and not to be told. But through it all and dealing with all of these various states and different culture of people thought me a lot. I have been able to see the world for what it really is, and get to know and meet people that I would never had crossed paths with. Everybody I met was for a purpose and was sent my way for a reason. We all worked together and we all got paid together. I have often been asked how did they get paid if they did'nt work, they still got paid even if they did'nt work for a month. I was in full control of this and that part was up to me to find them work. The condo and housing was all paid for and they had evrything that they needed there with them. They had to do nothing but sit and wait on my call. We all had the same plan, which was to make money and make as much as we could. Over the course of all of this I got more hoes coming in from evrywhere and in groups from all across the world coming to work for me. I tried to cover all 52 states if this was possible, but every state had different laws. Me and my organization aslo ran through and visited Las Vegas, Cuba, New York, and even Hawii. I was gifting hoes without even trying. Every town ciyt or state I was in or visted I was approached by someone that had heard about me and that was my in trough them. I had become worlwide on my own without walking the street a single day with a hoe. I was much different and my train of thought was much older than my years. I had hoes in all area codes and each hoe that would work for me would refer their friends and they would bring their cousins and so on down the line. Each girl that was being brought in would be fully examined and tested and tought the ten pimp and hoe commandments. Any of the ten commandments that was broken you would be asked to leave fo a year without pay and I would have someone else come in and take your place. There was always girls willing to work for me and I couldn't let one hoe ruin evrything I had going and had created because she did'nt know the commandments. They all had to learn and memorize these before they could work for me. My ten commandments were as followed. [number one] the hoe had to serve up to at least ten vicks or more a day. [number 2] they could never what he or she wants.[number 3] they were to give the vick oral sex for at least ten minutes or more upon the vicks request. [number 4] freak and have sex with the vick any way he or she wanted for ten minutes or more upon the vicks request. [number 5] never accept nay money or tips from any vick or for anything extra your time had already been paid for. [number 6] fuck and have sex with the vick to his or her max, don't stop until the vick is fully pleased.[number 7] always be ready and on time to meet with any vick, never be late. [number 8] please your vick anyway he wanted no questions asked, serve him well and keep him coming back for more [number 9] never get too close or attatch yourself to any vick this was just buisness. [number 10] strip, and dance for the vick however he or she wanted.striptease, bellydance, whatever to please the vick, no questions asked. These were my ten commandments one through ten and were to be followed out to the very end. I would have them learn them and them in one at a time, tell me, and explain one through ten to me before the could enter the work field. I called them all in and talked to them through a speaker phone bcause it was so many of them, like a class room. This was similar to a class because you had to pass this test before you could advance. These ten commandments was created by me to keep the vicks happy, keep the order, and keep me making money. I could'nt just send anybody out there without the proper guidence to represent me. I had to have order, nad rules to abide by and these were mine. I had too many hoes under me and had to have this for evryone that was in my organization. In my organization I also had women that were lesbians nad even men that was guy that worked for me I never missed out on any money. I may had not been into that way of life but other people was and I had request for them as well. One out of three of my vicks would request for one of them at any given time so I had to have them on standby when needed and the same rates apply. Meetings were held once a month, these metings were call the hoe and pimp meetings or the hoe and pimp meet and greet. At these meetings we talked about our buisness and what was our next city or town that we were going to next and how was going to tavel where. I switched up hoes and locations every so often to keep fresh faces around. At this time I also had their annual checkups that they must have. They would get an over all exame, and bring in the records with them for me to look over. This took place every month from each hoe that work for me, and they were all notified a month in advance for these meetings due to where they had to travel from. If for any reason they could not provide the proper medical report, or they could'nt make the meeting, they would be fined, or laid off for up until a year until further notice if they came back at all. I could not afford to take any chances on this, and give a disease to me or any of my vicks that requested a girl from me. The vicks medical records were also sent in bfore the hoe would arrive to them as well. I was held fully responsible for this. I was strick but fair, and I had to be. People trusted me and I had to show them that I could be trusted and truly run a buisness like no other, that was the reason I had so many hoes and so many vicks come to me over the others. They knew they were insured and everything was safe. A person needs to feel safe and that they can trust you and what you stand by is one hundred percent. In this life you have to stand for something or you will fall for anything. I remained undrecover for so long and had gained trust from all of my vicks worldwide because of my assurance that everything that was talked about remained confidental, and it was nothing was revieled, and whatever we talked about was just between us. I had one hundred percent assured that to each and everyone of them. I not only did this for them I did this for myself. I was so sure of myself and to prove that I stood by my word that I even had a return policy. Just like you see in stores when you go shopping, a money back guarentee if you were not satisfied, I ran the same kind of buisnes. I would return their money to them in full. So in order for me assure this did'nt happen I had to have a tight leash in the hoes to make sure they was on their jobs at all times. They always had to dress the part and remaine classy. I had to learn each and every hoe. I had to know what they could do how long she could do it and what she could'nt do. With this insight I knew each hoe personally and knew who to send to vick as soon as they called. There was a lot of sex involved but that was not what 1 was all about, but I still had to know what I had and what I was working with. All of my hoes were paid and well taken care of. They all received a pay check just like with ant other job. They got paid each month, plus what they made during the month according to how many vicks they had served. Each girl knew their role and they played it well. Just like with any other buisness you had your few that would mess up. When they realized what they had and what they would loose.

They straightned up real fast. I had hoes from all over and all of them knew that they could be replaced at any given time. Everywhere I went I had offers and was always in work and looking for the next batch. I never had to look far they came from across the world just to meet me. I kept maybe five to ten hoes on the side if need be. They were paid each month like everyone else even if they did'nt work. After six months if they were not needed they were free to go, the choice was up to them. I never forced a hoe to do anything, evrything was told to them upfront. Held back back nothing from them, a pimp has nothing to hide. This was'nt east and it was a step by step process. Each step had to be carried out, and had had to be approved by me first. If they were not up to my standerds they would be sent back until they got it right. This could take up to a couple of weeks to a month before the hoe would even hit the streets. There was a training process and rules that had to be met if you wanted to work for me. I never had to go out looking for hoes they flocked to me. Pimping has been around since before time and shows no sighn of stoping now. Some form of this has even been mentioned in the bible at some point in time, and will never stop. It's not always about what you do but how you do it. I was in buisness with some top notch people who could not afford to be cought or traced back to them, or me either for that matter. This was still prostitution and take down everything down that we had worked so hard to get. Some of them had more at stake then others. Some of them were lawyers, doctors, and had famlies that could not find this out. I stood behind them the whole step of the way and nothing was ever exposed. 1 had a hoe in almost every corner of the world, no matter where oyu went in the world their was someone there that worked for me. Once a month money would be collected an sent in, counted and distrubuted among us. I would take the sixty percent and divide the forty between them once a month plus however much they were paid in traveling at fifty dollars a mile. If the money was collected and distributed before that month was up, it was a good month and we called this a overload. This ment we had reached our limit before the month was out. I'm talking two million in just two weeks. I would go on to do this a few times. To honor the success we had throughout the year I gave annual hoe balls for all of my hoes. This was the opposite of the players ball. This was for good and hark work they put in for me, I covered all expenses and wnt all out for them cause I know they would have did the same for me. This was something I did'nt have to do, but I did it to show them my appriciation. The top five girls who did the best and earned the most money would all receive rewards, and a special bonus. For the ones who had not done so well were put on strike if word had got back that had not pleased the vick, or the vick had any complaints. If she was loosing money, she was costing me money. The penilty for this could have you put on the side for up til a year with no pay. The following year she would improve. During these hoe balls I invited drag queens to come in and entertain my hoes. They came in and danced,and performed for them. They put on a real good show too, and was paid well for this day. I paid them out of my pocket, all expenses on this day was covered by me. It was maybe five to ten of them that I would have come in on this day. This was every year that we had a hoe ball unless I decided to do something different that year. I did a lot for my hoes and would put my life on the line if need be. I even gave my hoes a bonus every Christmas for their good work even the ones that didn't. 1 treated them more like employees than like hoes. I was the boss, they were the employees, and the vicks was the clients. They put their lives on the line for me each and every single day they were out there, and I would do the same for them. That's how much they loved and respected me. They not only said it they showed it, and actions speak louder than words. They never received any abuse from me and I did'nt have to, a year off work without pay was punishment enough. They had to earn everything they got and nothing came to them without hard work. I was in the game too deep and could not afford for any of them to have my cover blown. I had ties with too many countries and I had money everywhere I never deposited it to banks only safty deposite boxes, then I started keeping hidden safes in our houses and hiding the rest in case we were ever raided. I have millions to come and go, as soon as it was gone or I hit rock bottom I would shoot right back to the top. It was nothing that was going to stand in the way of that. I have been there and done that over my years in the game and nothing comes as a surprise anymore. I was in the game for almost fifty years. I have come a long way from that seven year old boy that had nothing and was trying to hide who he really was. When I got over that I had become I was ment to be, a pimp. Once I got my own organization I vowed to never pimp an african american women again and that I did, don't take me wrong I am not a racist but I respected my sisters enough not to pimp them,an I never did again I received many offers from them to wor for mme but refused them all and explained to them my reasons for doing so, I recived even more respect for doing this. I also had no need to I had women from all around the world. With all this power and my own organization now I could do buisness the way I wanted now, I begain to transport girls across the border, where I would have someone meet them and bring them back. They would be paid and sent to get all of their identifacation changed saying that they were legal citizens of the united states. One of the first hoes that I met was from turin, italy and open up my eyes to a new side of buisness and she was my in. We went into buisness together and in just three days she had up to 200 girls willing to come to the united states and work for me. This open up the door for me to more forighn countries as well, this was my oppurtunity to become worldwide with this pimping and I jumped on it. Before arriving in the united states they would conduct buisness from there until I had everything set up here for them. I was back and forth at the time conducting my buisness, until one of my hoes was cought and my name got involved and I was found and sent back to the united states on the first thing smoking. Half of the women decided to stay unti things cooled down and the rest of them came back with me. They would still operate from Italy and send the money direcectly to me. After a month also things cooled down and I was able to send for the girls that had stayed behind and switch up every other month with a different rotation. This way it was always a new face around. We operated like this for a few years until the fbi got word of what we doing. I decided to shut down shop before it was too late and I lost everything. I was out of control, and then realized that I could not conduct buisness from over seas without any inside help I needed to be more hands on with this. I needed an inside person to handle this, someone from there, someone that I could trust. I had become bigger than I thought and had made a name for myself, one that soon everyone would know. I had almost become a household name. Now with this at hand I could'nt be seen as much as I used to. We worked hard for everything we had and partied just as hard, if not harder. We spent a lot of cash throwing these parties. But we never let the drugs stand in the way of the buisness that was at hand. Once fully back in the US I did'nt only spend money I made my money work for me and invested a lot of 1t into a bar and a lounge, which I also used as cover up's but also brung in a lot of money on the side. The bar was stationed upstairs as a fraunt for whoever walked in and downstairs was set up with rooms for the girls which lead to the back door. You could stop in for drinks and get some trim and be gone without anybody seeing you. I was always ahead of the game and was always thinking of ways to make money without being detected. Money was coming in from all around left and right, over a million dollars a day but that was'nt enough to split between 300 hundred people and still be able to make a profit. I needed more and I knew what I had to do to get it. More girls from over seas. When they came they would bring 2 or 3 of their friend and they would bring friends to join as well. Everbody knew my name but not by face because I was rarely seen if at all. The only time you would see me was when I was out and about on the streets trying to recruit more vicks for the hoes. Like I stated before I never walked the streets with any of my hoes.i used to hang with a lot of the pimps around this time, and it was funny to see how they operated. They would walk the streets with 10 to 15 of their hoes, and the whole time they did'nt even have a clue what I had under me worldwide. I was hustling right under their nose the whole time, they thought that I was just out there showing off and that's what I wanted them to think I never wanted the spotlight. This was one of the reasons I mananged not to get cought up on the streets with any of my hoes. Everybody knew me by name "caddy" was what I went by at the time. Caddy was what I went by on the north side. Chicago top dog was another one. Chicago top dog was I went by on the south side. Both names would be known to the streets and would follow me wherever I went I was international, no more local and had to be careful of every move that I made, it was no room for error in this buisness cause ine mistake could cost you evrything maybe even your life. Each name ment something and stood for something on the streets and I had earned them. Each name represented something. You either knew of me by ine of these names or just by percy. One way or another you knew me or of me, there was no doubt about it. A true pimp never needs or wants for nothing, all of his needs and wants should always be met. He is the leader and is in charge. The hoes are there to serve him and follow his command. I was born with leadershhip skills and used them well. This was something that I was born with and was tought by the best in the buisness, which only sharpend the instincts that I had inside of me the whole time. I can say that I lived my life to the fullest and had did and gone where no man has gone before. I was bigger than I had ever imagined, and was the only pimp or person for that matter with three or more names and they were all ringing in the streets like a payphone. I still don't know of any and have yet to find anyone else like me. I had the money power and the resect of everyone where ever I went and had my own organization. I was my own boss and never had to answer to anyone or ask for nothing during this period, I called the shots. I had started my own thing and everyone else was just trying to catch up. I was my own brand like pepsi, that's a brand mane I was a brand name. One of a kind, a true diamond in the rough. I sold myself first and foremost, never the other way around. Never walked the streets with anybody but myself, you had to go through me in order to get to them. This was just how I operated and that was how I rolled. I was the mastermind and the brains behind this organization all rolled up in one. I had the best of both worlds. I was always making moves and buisness transactions 24/7 seven days a week, rain, sleat, or snow I was out there selling myself for the hoes, the more vicks the more money. We were raking in the dough, i'm talking twenty to thirty thousand dollars a day combined with the hoes and the amount of drugs that they were moving had up in big buisness. What pimp you know or even heard of that can truly say that and mean it. This is one hundred percent truth from my mouth to your ears. This was big money and I have no regrets, and would'nt have it any other way. I st out to do this and set myself apart from what all the other pimps was doing or trying to do and be remembered for an eternity that has yet to come. I loved the life I was in and enjoyed doing it. It was fun for me even I knew this was not a game I still had fun doing so and I was making money while I was doing it. The fun part about it came to an end the biger I got and dealing with all of these different countries, started to stress me out. This was also the case with doing buisness from over seas, this was dangerous buisness, I never showed up in person or showed my face, cause I was not allowed in certain states. In order to do this I would send a girl already from that country that knew about the country and who was who. I would send her to get close to whoever the boss or head person in charge was and let her tell him what the plan was. If he ageed upon these terms then she would talk prices for more girls and fees for tranporting them across the border to the united states, then report back to me. I was very smart and played my hand-that I was delt 1n life, and never made excuses for anything, because eyrything in life happens for a reason. I had to be extra carefull and I had to be, cause any wrong move could have cost me my life. This was how I went about things, I was never seen but was well known for what I did. I always thought ahead and had a plan for everything to be played out. Transporting was where the big money was and 1 knew it, also was risky buisness but I was in it to win it. I had begain to ship up to 40 to 50 hoes a week, and got cought up with the drug cartel over the girls, money, and the amount of drugs that was being brought in at this time. I had a station on the north side where I conducted buisness from, but had to move around due to the amount of debt that was owed in turkey. Trying to reach the united states, but there was a time limit on this, and the rules was strick pay or die.so what was I my next move, there was a price on my head. I ended up going into hiding until I got up the money, because I feared for my life. When the money was made that we owed I set up a metting and place to meet to exchange the money, we were up to 2 to 3 million we owed at the time.in order to pay this off I had to flip what was left and double that just to stay in the game. It was sink or swim and I refuse to sink or give up now, I had come to far to give up now. We were getting taxed on every shipment that was being brought in. Now we were in buisness with Mexico, and the same rules applied trying to ship the girls across the border. But the money wasen't coming as fast as I thought in order to pay all of these expenses and meet their deadline. I got more girls, from china, turkey, russia, taihland, and mexico, more hoes and more debt. Had more hoes then ever I had 300 plus throughout the united states and over 500 world wide. This also put me deeper in distress, and started my addiction all over again due to the amount of stress I was under. I begain smoking heavyly just to relieve some of the pressure and take my mind off of what was going on and all the debt that we owed. This ment I had to work the hoes double in order for this to work, and to also save my life beacause It was pay or die no questions asked. This wayed heavy on me and sent me into a deeper state of dipression. I was still falling short after paying out all of this money and decided a quick way to make up the loose ends aws to deliver drugs to all of the drug boys through out the city to pay the remaining debt from over seas and keep me on top. I sold drugs and still ran the prostitution part of the game to cover 3 million dollars between 3 countries. Then begain to bargain with India and Russia to cover the remalng debt that was owed, and the price they had on my head. They wanted 10 percent off each girl as long as they were in the united states. This was their way of trying to control me, I never followed anybody elses rules I set the rules. I did'nt agree with this and decided to earn the money on my own the hard way. I turned to different loan sharks around the way to cover this. And had to pay them double the amount that was loaned oit which made me have to hustle harder and work the girls twice as hard this was to pay out what was owed and to supply my drug habit at the time. I also had over a million dollars invested in clothes for the hoes, beacause they had to dress to impress, letting the vicks know that they were top of the line and they were getting what they paid for. The more money that was being brought in the more money that was being spent, it takes money to make money. I still had ties with China, Russia, turkey and china, and with all these different cultures and different launges I had to pay an inturpitor to translate things for me and conduct buisness for me through them. During this time I was in hiding for nearly 3 years until the for each state was recovered and paid off. I had become a prisoner in my own home. When these 3 years was up, I was able to show my face again and walk the streets and a free man, and not having to look over my shouldr in fear of my life. With all of my debt cleared nad up to over 100 million dollars plus, I was bigger then I was ever before. It cost money to make money and to run an organization of this kind was never seen before, I'm talking 20 to 30 thousand a day, which came from over 29 hoe houses, various nite clubs lounges, and prostitution and not to mention security 24\7. There was cooks, butlers and a driver for the limo that had to be paid. Every where and everything we did we did in style and with class. Just another day in the life. After this I knew I had to shake this addiction and get back on my game this would be my down fall 5 to 6 times over my life spand and 1 bounced back from this every time bigger and bader than ever. Due to this I was forced to raise the price for each of the girls services, this increased up to 500 dollars an hour, plus the 50 dollars a mile they had to travel to the vick there and back. I selling to the higher class of people who could afford this such as doctors, lawers, presidents, and even movie stars who shall remain nameless. That's who had the big bucks and I knew this would put me over the top and give me the money and buisness

I needed. In this game evry person has to play the hand that he or she is delt in life, and I was playing mine to the fullest. I also know and believe that there is no man bigger than god and every man has a turning point and I was at that level to do so. I was always a thinking man, and always stayed ahead of the game, and was alwyays thinging outside of the box of bigger and better things that no one else was doing at this time. I always had a plan and carried out on everything I ever set out to do. I never received or asked for help in any of this pimping, I did all of this on my own that one the one thing about me. I was alone and I stood alone. The only other person who was in buisness with me was the queen bee. The money that was being made was spit among me and all the hoes was 60/40 1 would keep the 60 percent and give them the 40 percent, I'm talking millions. This was the wages I ran my buisness under and evryone was in agreeance and evrybody was making money, if you wase'nt then there was something you wase'nt doing.out of all this money that was being brought in over the course of this time, I never deposited any money into banks, and this was because they was able to trace this. I used safe deposit boxes all through this time. I also held meetings where we would all sit down and agree on everything that was an issue, and we would not leave until evryone was on the same page. There was so much money being brought in at this time I could'nt put all the safe deposit boxes in my name, so I started putting them in the hoes name and never had to worry about nothing. This was beacause my organization was built from the ground up off of trust and loyalty. In return I trusted them and they trusted me, so much so that I was willing to die for one of my hoes. I was not in love with any of them, I loved them all the same, they were all my lovers. There was nothing we had to hide from each other, and nothing we could'nt sit down and talk about like a true family, and that we was. I never had to hit any of them or come looking for anyone over all my years, because we all had an undrstanding and respect for each other. We were all on the same level and saw eye to eye on eveything we did. With this train of thought and undrstanding of the game I could not loose and refuse to loose, I was never a looser. My main goal in this this game was to show respect and in return I would get respect, from everyone from the police to the crack heads, and of course make money not only for now but the future and life after pimping. I also gave back as often as I could and still plan to do this. We were of a different class and carried ourself with respect and walked with our head high and never looked down upon anyone. I was and am truly one of a kind, the last of a dying breed, I was the mastermind behind all of this, and never showed my face but was well known without even being seen, and that's the way I liked it. That was also due to the amount of power I had. I never abbused the power I had, I used it to best of my abilty. I used the cards I was delt and never complaind about what I could not control! This was the same mind set I installed in all of my hoes as well, even to this very day. I would never try to harm them but better them and prepair them for what was yet to come, life after pimping. With this new found knowledge and out look on life and now my own organization I was able to make my own rules. I never pimped a under age girl that was my rule, every girl that worked for me was 18 and older, I am a real pimp to fullest and say that to say this I don't pimp the hoes I am a pimp to the hoes, that's the real meaning of a true pimp and that's part of the game that a lot of people and so called pimps and players don't know and I'm here to tell you that's not pimping. All my hoes had to also follow and abide by the pimp 10 commandments and this was tought to them upon there arrival to the organization, and was asked if they could handle this, if they could not they were shown the exit. These rules were my own and I planed for each one of them to be carried out to the fullest with no stones left unturned. Each hoe was tought the pimp and hoe 10 commandments and was given up to 6 weeks to learn and memorize the 10 commandments. If they did so they were worty to work for me in this organization. Once each of them learned and studied them it was time to work. No money was never transacted through the hoes but from the vick to me. They would also never travel with cash, I would send them with a credit card for their personal needs if needed. When I was contacted by the vick we would talk buisness and the amount of hours they wanted and what they were into. Also where they were to add the amount of miles they had to travel to reach them. I had cars for all of my hoes if it was driving distance or if they had to get on a plane, all this was totaled up. When evertthing was agreed upon, they would send the money directly to me. They would send it to my safe deposit box. Once the money was there is when I would send the girl or girls they had ordered, not a minute before. When the job was complete they would contact me and let me know they were on the way back. Then we would conduct buisness and how much she had made for this trip. I would subtract the expenses of the credit card and what was left was divided 60/40, plus their 50 dollars a mile they earned for the travel. This was the same for each hoe that worked for me, times 300 you do the math. Another one of my rules for those who haden't learned these 10 commandments, but still wanted to work for me had to pay upfront, never trust a hoe that did'nt know the Ten Commandments. I trained everyone of them, and told them what was expected of them and the job that had to be carried out, and could they handle it. Then that's when I might consider them. This still was not gaurenteed, I let a lot of them go do to this. If they could'nt please me they could'nt please the vick, the more the vick was pleased the more money he would spend. Without this proper guidence I would loose money and then be out of buisness due to this. One monkey don't stop the show. This rules was not only for the hoes but anybody that was under me. The head of the hoes is the queen bee her job was simple it was to find out through the 300 girls who did what and we would send them out upon request on what the vick had wanted, that is how we operated, and this kept everything running smoothly like a true buisness was supposed to be ran.everything has rules and laws and everything has an order of how things should go , you must have order and evryone has to be in agreeance for a buisness to run, without this you are only setting yourself up for disaster. I also made a major move in kansas, and masouri at the time as well. I never stayed in one spot for long due to the buisness I was in. Once the vicks had pretty much ran through the hoes I had in the area at the time, which was any where from 200 to 300 hoes in that city, town, or, state at the time. Once the vicks went through those it was time to switch up. I never let them get used to the same faces cause then the money would slow up, cause they did'nt want the same thing.' dressed to impress that was just my style,i never dressed like anyone else growing up. I tried to wear regular clothes like jeans and a t shirt like my brother, but it just did'nt feel right, that was'nt me. That's why I dreesed the way you see me. Over my pimping years I had 300 plus suits, all custome made, every suit represented something different. Every suit ment something,it wasen'nt just another pretty suit. Every suit came with the matching canes,hats, shoes, glasses, and socks they all represented something, and I had a different suit for every occasion, holidays u name it. I am one of the biggest pimps known to the world undercover, and that was because I walked the streets alone and sold myself not the other way around. Out of the 300 plus hoes that was under me at the time, they was stationed in different hotels and houses around the world, and they would'nt move until they got the word to do so,and I had a vick for each one of them.this was the same thing in all 52 states, I had hoes all around the world, I was world wide and had become bigger than I would ever had imagin. In Kansas I was also taken down, but I never served any time cause I would just pay it off. I paid one million dollars in cash to walk, I had the money to do this, and money talks. This was how I rolled and was never sent to prison over all my years in the game. Nothing could keep me down, I would get out and go right back at it straight to the top. The money was spent would be made back that very same day. I was truly one of a kind, I am no trick on any level, I'm 100 percent real. There was no love lost, so I returned to what I knew best which was pimping at it's finest. I started all over again with 300 plus prostitutes. At this time they just wanted me to lay back and let them run the buisness and deal the drugs, and continue to runnthe buisness for me and bring me the money, I would'nt have to lift a finger. Just as evrything was going good here comes the mobb. They were furious and ended kidnaping me due to the amount of money that I was making and the amount of women that I had under me. The reason they did this was because I did'nt need them anymore and they could not controle me anymore. They begain to feel threatened because I was becoming bigger than them, and they were the ones that tought me eveything I knew in the game. Like the saying goes more money more problems, and I had a lot of both, which often made me feel alone and this started eating at my concious and this is something i'm still dealing with this very day. It is almost as if I'm alone, like I'm the only one, which leads back to the title a pimp in distress, and this is very true. I never need for anything or needed for anything, because I took what I wanted and never had to harm anyone to do it. I am pure, and true to what I do. I was also shown support from the community, kids, and even police officers, which made things run smooth for me due to amount of support I was shown and I showed my love and support back. I had all 52 states covered, top and bottom and did'nt need anymore hoes at this point. I was satisfied with what I had, so why fix what's not broken, I was unlke anyone the world had seen, and ran my buisness the same, unlike no other, something the world had never seen before. To further prove this was the fact that I never sent my hoes to work the corner, you never seen me with a hoe walking the street, that was not me. I would sell myself to the customers who we called vicks, and they would tell me what they wanted and what they were into, and I would hand pick the girl for them upon there discription, and desire. Every vick was different and had diffeent needs, so in order to train the hoes I would have sex with all of them and show them the different ways and styles that they might be expected to do. And like I stated before I had my own personal doctor that would tie the tubes of evry girl that worked for me so they could not get preganat, I could not afford for this to happen due to the buisness I was in and they were told this upfront.by no means are my hoes tricks, we are all equal and we were as one , we were a team.i also would pay the hoes for there travel, 50 dollars for each mile they had to travel to each vick, and also what they were gitting from the vick for there services, whatever that may have been, like I said this a buisness and I ran it like a true buisness man.in the long run this would keep money in the girls pocket and keep the confusion down and keep us organized and ste us apart from anyone else that was in the pimping game at this time, there was none like us.we also never carried weopons as we traveled and made our moves, but get me wrong we were well protected at all times, don't get the wrong idea, this was just part of the game ew were in and was something that came with the territory. All the money we would collect we would all put in a bucket count it up and split it straight down the middle everyone got there fair share.they were not allowed to use drugs or get high unless there was a party being throwed that I threw for girls this was the only ocasion that was allowed no excecptions.the drugs the girls would carry were in too sets. There was a real pack and what we called a dummy pack, which was fake. They would sell all the drugs to the vicks, and pretend to get high to keep them spending more money. The more they pretend to get high the more the vick would spend to keep the party going. I had them well trained. This was in order for them to focous and to make as much money as they can and u can't do that when your high, then I'm loosing money and that was not the name of the game. there was also an age limit to hoeing and for me that was between the ages of 49 and 50 for my organization. When they reach that age I would send them into retirement, I had up to 100 hoes retire due to there age and I would start the hunt for a new batch of girls to bring in, and the traing process started all over again, I would train them and have their tubes tied as well and to see what they could do and could'nt do.this was the job for the queen bee to keep track of how many hoes was coming and going and keep track of the money flow that was being brought in. At this time I not only had girls I would pimp gays and lesbians as well, whatever the vick wanted I had it. My phone stayed ringing more than a hot line to the point I had to take sleeping pills just to sleep at night, this was big buisness. I had 300 plus hoes at the time and stayed get request from more and more girls but I had as much as I could handle and I started turning them down. And even through all of this I never lost a single hoe because I treated them all as an equal and we were a family. This is how I conducted buisness and I did it well, I was never the flashy type, I was never in the spot light, and I never made a scene. I was alsoconfroned by the vicks as well, not for the hoes but for me. This happened more than one time, I have been offered up to 500 dollars for them trick off with me, in this game nothing came as a surprise and that was just because of how I was dressed, who I was and how I carried myself, I was my own man , my own brand and never followed anybody else I made my own trends, and this 15 what set me apart from the rest.money will make peolple do some of the strangest things,,the type of things that you can't imagin in your wildest dreams.' noticed this in my own family towards me. I was offered sex from my own family, just for the fast life and the lifestyle they wante. In the end I refused. This is not cause they was family, but because they were not on my leavel, not of my standerds to work in my organization. I seen nothing in them that would make me money and I knew I would be unable to sell them to any of the vicks that was involved with me, cause all of my hoes were of a certain class, a certain level. I did find other ways to use them, I would use them on the drug side of things, and in return I would fraunt them drugs and they would bring me the money. I even sold them one of my cars to transport and move the drugs. This worked out for a while until the car broke down and so did they,soon they were raided for selling drugs out of there house and everything was down hill from there.some of them are still strugglig with addiction to this very day, the others have moved on and made a life for themselves. During this time to keep my buisness in order every month I would hold a pimp and hoe meeting each month to let every one know what was there task and where they would be placed, and during all of my years in the pimp game I never lost a hoe and never cought a disease from any of them I guess u can say I was lucky because I know a lot of pimps who did. After I got well or at lease I thought I was I was right back at it, this time with twice the amount of drugs and up to at lease 29 hoe houses at the time. I thought I was smarter than the game and could not be touched, that was not true.I began to take some of out of the packs they were suppling me with and giving it to my friends and crew in other words I was playing both sides making double the money, until that day it all cought up with me, like the saying goes what goes around comes around. I was lurred and tricked into the home of the druglords who then forced me into the basement where I was striped of my clothing and streatched out across a pooltable with 5 golf balls shoved up my ass, beaten with a baseball bat, and stabed in the chest with a 10 inch butcher knife, when yhey realized I was still breathing they then drove me to 31st street beach where they then dumped my body and I was left for dead. I was later discovered by man that was jogging past and noticed something floating in the water and alerted the police.i was dead on arrival, but heard a voice speak to me. I was in acoma, for 6 months and was later told what had happen, and the condition I was in and that my life would never be the same. Deep down inside of me I knew this was it and the end was near for my pimping days, but I did'nt listen. They say listen to your first mind for a reason and I did'nt. Shortly after I was approached by an fbi agent and he told me they were watching me, because my name had become so big they were hearing about me across the world. My mother pleaded with me and asked me to move back with her, but I was in too deep. That was my warning but I didn't listen they soon raided my house again but I pleaded with themm to let the girls go, and in return I would take the charges if I agreed to tell them where everything was, which I did, from 10pounds of weed, herion, guns, and over 20 million dollars in cash,29 cars I mean everything.upon arriving in court I was suggested to cop a plea deal nad agree to all the terms then I would'nt have to face a long jail time, because I was looking at over 65 years if convicted on all charges. I agreed and they ceased everything in order for me to wlak and my name was cleared of all the charges and record was cleared of all charges and remains clean until this very day, and now had a fresh start and a clean record. But now

I was left with nothing, back to the drawing board. Once again I was back homeless with nothing I had hit rock bottom which lead me back to the drugs, stealing and whatever I had to do at that time to get some money. this was something I never wanted to experience, but I was down and out, no money, staying from shelter to shelter, eating out of garbage cans. I was down bad, during this time I stayed with a few of my kids who supplied me with drugs as well, they had become my dealer until my money ran out, then they had no use for me anymore and treated me like another customer instead of their dad, and I entered myself into drug rehab. Shortly after the girls found me and put me right back into the game, because they did'nt want to work for anyone else and they did'nt like the condition they saw me in. Soon I was back on top and everything like I never left, and them came mansions, money, cars, jewerly, and anything I wanted and this time I planed on staying there. With all the connects I had the drugs were easy to come by, so I started working with a connect through texas, and told him I wanted a fresh start and he sent me double of everything.in order for me to stay clean I had the girls to opperate the drugs and they brung me the money, but soon became depressed do to the lack of involvement withh the drug game. And I wonder why this was napping to me I supported the one around me with no love in return. I received no letters or phone calls of support or encouragement from any of my family during my time of need. Have gave back as much as I could, I donated to several churches, and to red cross gave out turkeys on thanksgiving just to give back

,i've even threw houndreds of dollars out of car windows just driving down the street to the kids just trying to give back and show my support to the people that had shown love and support for me throughout my years in the game. But all good things come to an end, my name started ringing in the streets again, and I had become bigger than before every time I had a stepback I always bounced back bigger and better then before, as soon as you counted me out is when I came back for the top and here comes the fbi and evrything was ceased for a second time. Now I'm back with nothing and no one. I was sentenced to a drug rehab apartment where I would stay until I got clean.upon me leaving me and my hoes decided to just stop dealing with the drugs and just stick to the prostitution. This worked because of who I am. And then I became so big I thought I was bigger then the law and felt untouchable caues of the money that was being made there was no amount that I could'nt pay and make back that same day up until 1985. In just two years later in the fall of 87 my health begain to fail and I had to step back a little. This was something money could'nt fix so I decided to play behind the scenes this time, until the year of 1993 I started a few buisnesses of my own, which included a lounge, nite clubs you name it, money was still being made but this still did'nt fell right to me, something was still missing, then I realized I was missing the pimp game. This was what I had been custom to for long and all I knew, this goes all the way back to my early childhood and out of all the jobs I had throughout my life nothing seem to fit me but pimping so I took that as this what I was meant to do. Unfortauntly I was forced to stop due to my illness and health issues over the years and shortly after suffereed a massive stroke, and was also treated for epalepse and spent the next 3 weeks recovering, and was told by the doctors that I would not be the same, and was unable to work. That's when all druglords and pimps all begain a drug war and I knew I was next because of who I associated with I was shot 17 times from this but I did not die. 5 years later I was back in the pimping game again , after my comeback the FBI raided all of dope houses and I was taken to jail where I had to plea bargin in order to walk they took evrything, after that I had to start over in 1990 in drugs and sells again, after that I begain to get sick and ill due to the multiple gun shot wounds, and all my hoes continue to prostitute and sell my drug even though I was ill, and in 1996 I was discharged from the rehabilitation center, there I met a girl from my home town once I was discharged she took me home with her, by her not using drugs herself she was able to help me not to use drugs again and helped me stay clean, and who knew this would be the women that I would marry, shorttly after we got married but it would'nt last, the marriage only lasted 3 months because I was never a one women man, this was something new to me and I coulnd't handle it. To this day I still think back and the real reason I think got married was the way I thought I was supposed to live, life of a normal person I thought, to settle down and have a real family. there was no real love in this marriage, over the period of this time she had become verbal and physcially abbusive toeards me. Do to my illness I was unable to defend myself and in my opinion I was being kicked while was down.even pushed into a door while I was in my wheelchair but still tried to do for them. All these things I did out the kindness of my heart for the people I loved and thought they loved me back but that was not the case. During this time I always reached out and tried to help my family until I realized that wase'nt there for me in my time of need unless I had money they wanted evrything right now. they never saw the big pitcher of what I was trying to do for them, which was set them up for the long run for them and there kids, kids down the line. I would also offer buisness ventures to my kids for the future, but the still wase'nt satisfied including my ex wife whom I tried to open up a rehabilitation center for, car washes for the kids all of this with no regards.' would also help her side of the family in there time of need 500 to 600 dollars at a time and they all turned there back on me. In my eyes this was some type of jealousy or hate they had against me and I could'nt understand why. When I was up I had it all and everybody around me was happy as long as the money was coming in, they did not have to earn anything. When I fell down they were no where to be found, I was left on my own. I lived a rich man's life and everthing that came with it. I also lived a poor man's life too. I had the cars, the furs, the clothes, and the hoes came with it. I was always quick on my feet as well and always was a thinking man, I was always thinking of what's next to expand my organization. I had homes all over the place, every where I was, because I never stayed in one spot for too long. I never setteled in one place or got comfortable with anything. Once my job was done I was gone. I'm still like this to this very day. When I go out I show my face and my support and I'm gone. I was and am a smart man with no education but had common sense and strret smarts. With all this money I did'nt just spend it I made my money work for me, I made my money make money, I was making money in my sleep. I invested a lot, nad open up many buisnesses opertunities for a lot of people in my family for them to have something and better themselves I was always thinking of ways of giving back and helping those in need. I had my own rehabilitation center in my name for my ex wife to run built from the ground up. All of this buisnesses they let go down and the rehibiltation center was soon bought by the state and is now a tire shop. They did'nt take advantage of what I was trying to do for them. They were not in there right mind, and did'nt see what I saw, and let the drugs take their attention away from the buisness that was at hand. This would happen several times of the course of my life trying to help others that did'nt want to help themselves. I had a lot and I gave back a lot. Each time I got married I was running away fromm who 1 really was. I wanted what everyone else had and everybody wanted what I had. Each time I got married I held a meeting and told my hoes that this would be it for good, bu they knew better and tried to talk me out of it every time. Each marriage would only last from three to four months tops. Each time I left it was like the hoes knew it wouldn't work and continue to run the buisness as if I as still there. I tried so hard to prove them wrong, and each time

I returned bigger and better than before. While I was gone I was in deep distress and could not live a normal life as a normal family man. Each time I got divorce and was gone at the drop of a dime, but I never negleted the kids. The main reason for this was not the money, cause I had enough of it to get out at any time, it was the trill of the fast life style. But I always wanted the one thing I could'nt have which was a family but I knew this was not the life for me. I am a pimp and will be a pimp til the day I die. All of my kids know me as their father and later in life they all tracked me down, all 24 of them. I am a great father just not a family man. I always and will always be a pimp it comes like a second nature, it's in me to be this way and was from the very beginning. I kept proof and have documents and proof of evrything to this day. This is only to show you what i'm saying is true, and to prove the fact that family will do you worse than a stanger. Starting from 1997 due to my illness and various health issues I went down and started getting real sick up until 2000. This was the year that I knew I could not continue and my health begain to get worse. Starting in 2000, I was released from another nursing home due to my health and drug abuse, I started living out a hotel cause I had no where else to go. I would stay there until I was able to get back on my feet, and I could save money for my own house or apartment this way. Staying there I ran into my ex wife eho was staying there as well, and was there doing the same thing I was doing and suggested that we put our money together and get a place together. I had a bad feeling about this but did it anyway because she had a young daughter with another man and I did/nt want to see them live like that. I paid for over half of all the expenses, and carried the load for the most part, because she had previosly filed for bankruptcy. This is when I noticed they had no food, and this I bought as well. She also had a son that was 18, that I loaned money and help support from time to time too. I covered as much as I could to help them. I paid the bills, got her out of debt, and tried to support her two kids that wasen't mine, paid gas bills and the water bill at this time that was over six hundred dollars. This was not part of the deal upin moving in I could have done all of this on my own in my own place. She worked at a nursing home at the time but wase'nt making much money so I covered her, and picked up the slack until she got a better paying job to support her and her two kids on her own. This broke me cause I was paying for all of this out of my social security check each month. I also co sighned a car for her so that she could get around and find a higher paying job, which she did. That's when the tables turned and was starting to treated as if I wasen't neede anymore. I felt used and hurt because I was doing all of this cause all I wanted was a family and thought that they would be that for me. This only put me more in distress, also cause I was trying to be something that I was not. A family man, a single women man, I was not used to this, and this was something totally new to me. After all of this and how they treated me I still did for them. I opened up checking accounts in her name and her daughter name for them to continue to live and for her daughter when she turned 18 she would have something to afll back and finish school. I stuck this out for nearly six years until 2006 when I moved out and was accepted into the lower income housing. This is where I am still living to this day. She went her serparate way and I did the same. Over the years we still remain in contact and speak to each other on a daily basis. When I talk to her now she often thanks me for what I did and what I aws trying to do, she now sees for herself. Now on my own I tried to start fresh and forget all about my past life, but it still haunts me. To deal with this I was invited to speak at different organizations and groups as a motivational speaker. Whenever I would be asked I would do so, in order to help someone else as well as myself get through this. During this time my ex wife had been in a car accident, she called me and I helped her purchase another car a 2008 chevy, which she still thanks me for. To this day she is doing well and is on the right path in life and I wish her nothing but the best. I decided to call all of my hoes in and announce them the news and what was going on. I threw a real big party for everyone that was involved with me and let them know I had to give this all up. At this point I let them know that I was through and they were on their own, but I did not leave them empty handed. All the money that we had up until that point and the money we had put up was divided amoung us. Do I still miss the old times, of course I do, but my health want let me continue. Some of my hoes still stay in contact with me and stop by to see me every now and then to this day. Wll my health issues are being treated, all of my debts are paid off and all of my hoes are well off. I have been able to live off of social security from 94 to 2006.1 am telling you this for you to better understand me and to know where I'm coming from. I have been undercover for so long, it feels good be free, and be able to talk about my life. This is a big help. It took a lot out of me to prepair this book but I am still under a lot of pressure, but through it all I never gave up and I never threw my hand in or gave up on what I wanted out of life and I am living proof that you can over come anything. Over the time in the game I learned a lot and became so big and had so many hoes under my following my every command, I saw a bigger pitcher in what I was doing and begain to ship and transport these women to various places and to different people some even famous who ever had the money. I had a prostitue ready to take them for everything they had and in return they would sell themselves and the drugs 1 would send with them.' even had women sent to the white house, pesidents, movie stars, everything was confidintial, classsified and I would go to the extreme to cover them in any way from them or me getting cought because we both had something at stake. Whoever requested my services I would assure them this. Whoever was in need of my services I had a girl for them. Any time day or nite any where in the world I had them. I became so big and so good at what I did I had them by request just name it and I had a women for it. At this time I was making so much money it was scary 25 to 50 thousand a day the amount of money you can only dream of and I was making that in a day, 365 days a year no days off. There was no sick days in this buisness cause when your sleep somebody else is making the money, pimping will never die. But that was just the start of my problem and the money could'nt solve it, this only stressed me out even more, because the fact still remained that I was still alone and own my own the true meaning of a pimp in distress. throughout this time the hoes never left my side, found me no matter where I was, and refused to work for any one else, I could'nt even give them away if I wanted to, they said hell no and contiue to follow my every command, sell the drugs and bring me the money no questioned asked, and due to this I never wanted for nothing and I did'nt have to hit or hurt anyone to do it, unlike this so called pimps you see today. I never had to track any of them down, threatened them in any form of fasion. I had become my own, my own name, my own brand and the fact remains you can't undo me, I will be a pimp until the day I die. So I continue to do what I knew best, I was like a celeberty a true legend in my own right to the point you had to make an appointment or ask for me by request to even meet or hold a conversation with me. At this point I was ahead of the game, followed my own rules, and this was the I chose to live with no regrets.with the game comes pain and that goes without saying, the true testimoney of a pimp in

distress. After that I moved out and to my own home in the low income housing, so with this came benefits from the state and received a settlement later that year in 2006, following the next year I relacated to the lower income housing. With this I now knew that it was offically over and that it was time for me to give it up for good, but the pimp in me will never die. After I came to terms with the fact that it was all over I was still beind cotacted by some of the former hoes which did'nt make my decision any easier, they still wanted to work for me and wanted me to be there pimp, but I refused. I had experianced life to the fullest and had been from the bottom to the top and back again, left for dead and yet I'm still here, so god must have some greater for me. Through this all I was tired and needed to release some pressure, clear my concious, and repent for all of my sins and wrong doings I have done throughout my life. I soon begain to have nitemares and flashbacks of my life which I still have til this very day. In my sleep at nite I can see my life lke it just happen yesterday in the back of my mind. Talking about it and just thinking about it brings back so many memories. Now I am taking various medications and has to see a counseler and a theripist do to this. So I decided to give my testimony not only for me but for the world, and maybe my story can help another person who is headed down the wrong road and think that this came easy you are sadly mistaken, I went through a lot to get to where I am today. Now I see the bigger pitcher and tried to use my knowledge for good this time and talk to the children letting them know the ins and outs of the game straight from my mouth to their ears, and let them know what could happen to them if they choose this life. I strongly suggest you to not try this at home. To this day I am not pimping anymore and want to share my testimony with the world, the kids and whoever cares to listen so they can see for themselves that pimping aint easy and this is a rough life and is not for everybody, and that family will sometimes do worse than a person you don't even know upon writing this book as well as the documenery I reached out to evryone about to see what they thought and to get all the support I could through this, I have received nothing. I have 24 kids in total throughout the world and have reached out to all of them with no response. I had previously written a will out to distribute all of my worldly possesions, money, furniture, all to the state, but soon will have that changed and put only the one person who helped me through this. This is my hosekeeper maurice who has helped me a great deal through this, and encourged me to continue on with this, I was in doubt many times and thought this was not a good idea, but had a change of heart and decided all that I have been through the world deserves to hear this, I am here for a reason and I now know it was through the blessings of the lord. This is a note to everyone that has written me off I will always remember what you did and did'nt do, no hard feelings, no love lost that's just the way it is. I also decided to write this book of my life, trials and tribulations I went through and then maybe you can better understand why I am the way I am, a pimp in distress. I am not a pimp now, but I will always be a pimp at heart and a pimp until the day I die .there is no changing that. with that being said I strongly suggest to all readers and listeners of this to not try this at home I have lived it and I'm here to tell you by experience this is not the life for you, I am one of the last evryone else around me at the time are dead and gone so god must have bigger and better things for me in store and I know that's true bcause of all I've been through I'm still here and I hope this reaches someone and hope I will change someone life. Have come a mighty long way from having nothing no clothes or socks on my feet I never gave up, I never gave in and I am happy to say that I am drug free to this day and I contiue to live life everyday with no regrets. After it is all said and done I would like to give back to various charities and to help support the kids and show them that there is a better was and to give them hope and all the support that I did'nt have, that is my purpose for this book. To give hope to the community and the kids for the future, then I know I have done my job. If this book can reach someone if not but only one person then I know that I am doing the right thing. 1n return I don't expect nothing but a clear mind and maybe I can live the rest of my life in peace without all of the preasure weighing me down , that is the main purpose of this and for you to fully undrestand why I titled the book as such, a pimp in distress. This is how I feel and the life I lived. My pimping days are long gone, but never forgotton. Now i'm just enjoying life and living as a true testimoney to the world and to save the children, I am retired and i'm doing this to represent the struggle I been through, my childhood I never had, and for you to better understand me, and why I am the way I am. I never blamed anyone for nothing and realize that everything happens for a reason in life. From nothing to something, with no education and yet I still made it, and if I can do it, you can do it as well. Never through your hand in on life, because then that means your giving up and I never did that, and if you do so you are a looser in life. If I did I would'nt be here today. As of this year 2015 I am still not pimping and live alone and on my own I am blessed to be here today and still get love and support from evryone I speak to and never have I got any bad or neggative feedback from anyone. When I walk the streets now I am like a celeberty. From those that knew me to the ones that have heard about me, to those who have yet to read about me. I still dress up in some of the suits and show off to the people from time to time, when my health allows me to do so. This makes me feel good, and causes a lot of attention when I step out I have even caused accidents from this, everybody stops me and shake my hand and to take pitchers of me soon as I step out of the front door. I'm just remembering the times good and bad. The life of a pimp is very lonely as well as the life after. Life after pimping you are a loner and your all alone. The area I live in stresses me out at times, because there is nobody around on my level, and nobody here to fully understand me. I have no one to talk to about different situations because there is no one on my level or have been through what I have been through, which makes it hard to relate to. This only leads me to more stress for me. I now have cousenlors and theripist come to my house on a daily basis to help me through this. This is a step by step process. I still have all of my original suits and clothes all 300 plus that I still wear whenever I go out. I have old documents and tapes of my pimping days. To this day I have yet to run into anybody like me around where I stay which makes them hard to relate to. Due to my current health issues I am unable to travel and move around as much as I used to, or travel to where some of the older pimps and players of my time are. There isn't that many if any that made it to the point I am today, most of them are dead and gone or strung out. This leaves me in the mindset that I am alone. Due to the accident and head trama I still have flashbacks as clear as day in my sleep, but now I can see what is yet to come, maybe it's a gift and a curse. I now have a house keeper, home nurse and doctor that comes out and treats me for my illness, monthly doctors visits and they all congradulates me on my progress and how far I have come, I take it for what it's worth, I have my good days and bad days like expected but I can't complain, and that god that i'm still here. My kids check on me from time to time over the phone and some come to see me. I have almost fully recovered from my stroke a few years back nad can now move around on my own. I can talk without sluring and I'm just thankful. This is a condition that I know will never leave and i'm just fighting every day. Some days I feel weak and use my eletric chat to move around and on my good days I walk around the neighborhood. Every other month or so I still visit one or two of my clubs that are still around, just to show my face, my love, and support to those that were around me at that time. In return they do the same for me. They visit me, bring me gifts and still honor me. I am still treated like I was the day I left pimping, I am treated like a king. The choices I have made have brought me a long, long way and would like to thank the people, and most importingly god, cause without him I would not be here, never give up, never give in, follow your dreams, be a leader and never a follower and be all you can be. Is the message that I want to send with this book. I have tried to tell and show you the life of a real pimp and my trails and tribulations I went through on this journey called life. I did'nt choose this life it chose me. I didn't enter this game for the fame, money, or glamour. It was the life I believe that I was ment for me. My family was all in the buisness, my mother a hoe, my father, and my uncle were pimps, so what do you think that I would turn out to be. Growing up as a child you always wonder what is your purpose on this earth or in life. I tried my hand in different fields of life and various jobs, and none of thim seem to fit me or felt right as I was doing them. The problem was not that I was'nt good at it, but I knew that it was'nt ment for me. I tried for so long to fight it, but it would not let me. I never got in this buisness to hurt or harm anyone, that's the reason I have been around for so long, and have received so much love an respect over the years from everyone I have come across. I treated everyone with the same amount of respect that was given. Too much is given, too much is to received. Real recgonize real and I never sugar coated nothing, I told it like it was. Upon writing this book it was like a dream and still is. I never thought this day would come to pass, I did'nt think that I would be here today able to tell my story do to the life I was living. I believe in god but I was never a god fearing person, but with all I have been through nobody else could have brung me this far but him, and I would like to thank him for that. I am truly blessed to ave a second chance on life. I have had several, and plan to use it wisely. I plan to use all of my knowledge and wisdom I have for good this time. Maybe I can even change the world, but you cant change the world until you change yourself and your out look on life. I plan to do everything legit and by the book to prove that I am real about what i'm saying. This is the truth. I refuse to settle for less. I am here to serve a higher purpose in life and use this newly found knowledge to the best of my ability, because I might not have another to do so. This 100 percent real life and the facts of a true pimp in distress. Pimping is not for fun nor is there a class to teach you this, I happen to be brought up in this, and had to face the fact of what I was and yet to become. I rolled with the punches and inbraced it. There is only so long you can hide who you really are. I am unlike no other man or woman in this day and age, and yet to find anyone like me anymore. Everyone that was around me at that time aer all gone now and I am the last one standing here today to tell about it. I have been shot 17 times, stabed, golf balls up my rectum, beaten with baseball bats and left for dead.when everybody else around me got stabed or shot once and died. I have come way to far to give up now. The last of a dying breed, one of a kind, one of the greatest, a living legend, are just a few of the names I have been called, and underneath all of this I am still a man, born alone, and still I stand alone. Now with this unerstanding you can undrerstand who I am, and what I am and understand why I titled the book as such a pimp in distress. I could have not put it no other way. This is my story, my life, my heartaches, and pain, my testimony, this is me the untold story of a true pimp of this life style, and what I went through to get to this point in my life. A true pimp, a hundred percent all of me, a hundred percent real, the whole truth and nothing but the truth from the one and only Chicago top dog. I offically retired from the game in 1994, and thought I was well enough to return in 2000. With all of my health I could not continue. I have been in and out of the hospital and could not keep up with the pimping game. I have still received request from girls to work for me but I turned them all down. I had to face the fact that I am in no condition to run an organization as I once did. I was a young boy when I started in this buisness, and once had it all. I had all the world had to offer. I had to struggle to reach the top and had to fight to stay there. I have beat all odds and got over my addiction of drugs at least six times over the course of my life. I had more to do, and I knew there was something greater for me to do. This was my first step in writing this book. I now have a second chance to reach the top, leagally and legit. I also have a documentery based on my life also, and plan on making a part two in the making. I have watched my other pimps documentery and stories and they were all missing something. They were all missing to inform the kids that this is not what to do, instead of showing them the bright side of things. With my life story and my documentery I plan to show them the down side of things and what could happen to them if they chose this life. I want to let the kids now that there is nothing good in this and to stay in school and get their education. It is only two choices that can result in this life and that is dead or in jail. There is very few that make it out and live to tell about it. I am one and want to use my voice to reach and change someone elses life for the better. I have always been generous and gave back to my people. I love the kids and try to talk to them every chance I get. I have threw parties for them and always try to say anything positive to encourage them. Some of them have no one to tell them this. Kids need to hear this, just as a reminder that that do anything they set their mind to. They still love and respect me very much. When they see me they all run up to me, shake my hand, give me hugs and some even take pitchers with their phones. They may have not been around to personally know me, but see how I dress and 1 don't want them to get the wrong idea about me. The police officers all show me the same amount of respect when they see me. They stop and wave, some even stop their cars in the middle of the street get out of the car just to take a pitcher with me. Evrywhere I go I am stoped, from the moment I walk out the door I have people stoping me or talking to me about something. I always stop to them and speak, because of the respect that they all show me. Some of them may not fully know me or understand me but they respect me and that's all I can ask for. I always show love and support to everyone and got the same in return. I am very thankfull for everything, for the good and the bad, but I am still here as living proof of a pimp in distress. I wold like to thank everyone that took out the time to listen to my story and to read this book. I hope this book touches something in you to do better than me, this is a message to the world, not only the kids. From yours truly, the one and only Chicago top dogg. In the mean-time you can purchase this book, a pimp in distress, you can also purchase the documentery titled Chicago top dog 1.

Coming soon the follow up documentery part 2.
P.s. thank you for all of your love and support.

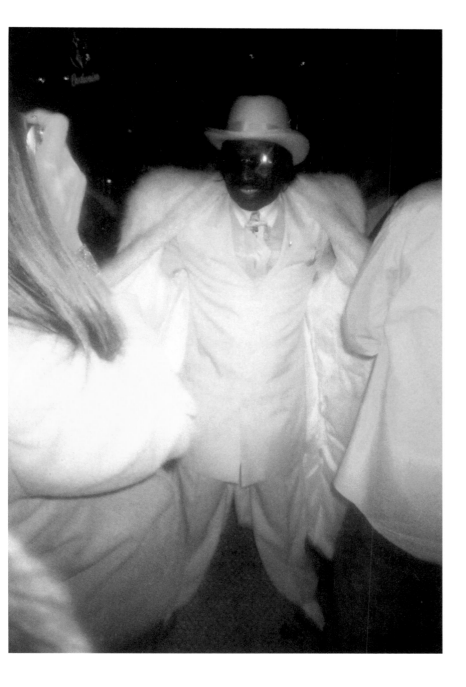